Also by Rod Usher

Poetry
Above Water
Smiling Treason
Convent Mermaid

Novels
A Man of Marbles
Florid States
Poor Man's Wealth

Non-fiction
All You Ever Wanted to Know About Sleep But Were too Tired to Ask (with Ron Tandberg)
Images of Our Time (Press photography, with Bruce Postle and John Lamb)
Their Best Shots: 21 Years of the Nikon Awards

Rod Usher

The Bare Hook

For James Button and May Lam

The Bare Hook
ISBN 978 1 76109 285 5
Copyright © text Rod Usher 2022
Cover image: Eva López

First published 2022 by
GINNINDERRA PRESS
PO Box 3461 Port Adelaide 5015
www.ginninderrapress.com.au

Contents

Blood	9
Don't it Always Seem to Go	10
Common Ground	11
Japanese Clock	13
Time	14
Climate	15
Desert Island Words	16
First Hotel	18
Foothills	21
If Not More	22
Ingredients	24
Personal Geometry	25
The Hunter Home from the Hill	27
The Imperfect	29
Gained in Translation	30
Pursuit	31
Sestina	32
Losing, Lost	34
Optional Third Lines of Five Syllables	35
Nudged	36
Partners	37
Refreshed	38
High Church	39
Seconds Before	40
Out of Mind	41
Wanted (I)	43
Wanted (II)	45
Petra Garcia Prieto's 100th	46
Fontaine	47
The Third Eye	49

The Origin of 'Marital Bliss'	51
Turdus merula	52
Dished	53
Ode to Red	54
Last Train	55
The Corpse Position	56
The Dark Side	57
The Mind's Cession of its Kingdom	58
On the Road to Barcarrota	59
Typing World War II Letters	60
Onward Soldiers	63
Marginal Notes	64
Roll Over Bing Crosby	67
Chutzpah	68
Epithalamion	69
Swifts	71
Walking Out of Tomorrow	72
Babylon and Everywhere	73
Turn, Turn, Turn	75
Ducks	76
Flight Fright	77
Verde que te quiero verde	79
Room with a View	80
Let There Be Dark	81
Word	82
Fifth Wheels	84
Monody for Maria	85
Broken Secret	87
500 Million Reasons	88
Haiku for the Dead	89
Pantoum	90
Overburden	92

Villanelle	93
Father	94
Preparatory	97
Una Domenica Qualsiasi	98
Separation	99
Addiction	100
Bittersweet	101
Homage to Flat	102
Spreadeagled	103
Not Counting	105
Not	106
Diminuendo	107
Coming Back as a Bird	108
Acknowledgements	110

'… Australian poetry is as profane as often as it is sacred; there is a rich vein of irony and satire that runs through our poetics, a colloquialism, contrarianism and playfulness that separates it from its counterparts in the northern hemisphere.' – Sarah Holland-Batt, editor, *The Best Australian Poems*, 2016

Blood

Like air, it has no given shape.
I guard mine tight within thin skin,
the way one clingwraps food to keep
it from spoil or spill.

Cuts or tears let the creature out,
a stream overflowing its banks.
Freed, it won't be led back again,
likes to run away.

It will soak a white shirt stop light,
darken dirt drop by dying drop,
etiolate strength to leave a
whiter shade of pale.

Some shadows of the past course it,
Blood's Blood says the cliché tattoo,
meaning alcoholic granddad
may revisit you.

It plays to a musical score
– systole, diastole, *non troppo* –
a concert without conductor,
never an encore.

Don't it Always Seem to Go

Hadn't noticed that I hadn't noticed
they are no longer pestering High Street,
under café tables, or, given the chance,
up on them stealing, ahop, ahop.

Far plainer than feted hawks and falcons,
loquacious lyrebirds, diva magpies,
they wear the camouflage of city grit,
their one-note song as cheap as chips.

Small as the redbreast, the rarer redstart
but lacking poetry's florid lobby,
they could boast having the numbers,
until their numbers started going down.

Distorted seasons and particled air
in their tiny chests have made them, at last,
significant: if this crumby lot dies,
what hope for bees in the modified corn?

If they fall from the sky and cityscape
hawk and falcon also loosen their grip,
and what once seemed to be idle gossip
we'll miss. Like that oak before the car park.

Common Ground

The father I never knew has no grave.
Someone from a funeral parlour
placed him without love
 – which is fair enough –
into some state-owned hole
at the huge Springvale Cemetery.
As an adult I asked Records
about unclaimed ashes,
was told that after x years
they go to common ground.

I'm glad it wasn't his flesh and bone.
Father was killed in a car crash
two thousand miles away from Mother
and we three children.
She couldn't confront his reduction
from man to urn.
I was four at the time but as we grew
photos had to substitute headstone.

Decades later I placed a son's ashes
from a Tupper-like container
a parlour had provided
into a fine box brother-in-law made.
They travelled the world
with me and his mother for years.
At airports, security always required
the Death Certificate.
I'd tuck Damien under the seat
for take-offs and landings.

It was his mother's call, I am his step
 – I still hug tight the present tense –
and after many years she decided:
a garden bed at the village house.
A windless day, we shared the pouring.
Now when I water, I think of him
so diluted
yet still so solid in my heart.
When the house is sold,
mother and me up some other chimney,
his siblings in a shortening queue,
what of him, forever 20, will remain?

Damien was a serious cat lover.
When our stray marmalade died
I buried Murci not far from him
beside a rosemary bush.
On my sunnier days I try to forget
the English burial service,
imagine one spirit stroking, one purring
in their common ground.

The English burial service is prefaced with this, in red: 'Here is to be noted, that the Office ensuing is not to be used for any that die unbaptized, or excommunicate, or have laid violent hands upon themselves.'

Japanese Clock

Each hour a small door
opens and a little bird
chimes 'Haiku! Haiku!'

Time

'In my day,' rants the
old man, as though he'd only
had 24 hours

Climate

Winter hands on your
bottom in bed, a lesson
in global warming.

Desert Island Words

A mere ten to save and savour. Tougher than discs,*
where Ludwig, Wolfgang, Leonard…auto-choose.

Añoranza, the homesickness all Crusoes suffer,
the Spanish gentler, more heartfelt, not at all bilious.

And *libélula*, Spain's due elegance to the dragonfly,
flameless four-winged ace who mocks the Harrier jet.

France's *Camembert* to allow a laugh on hungry lips:
the perfect cheese…how came it to be a Bert?

Also soft *souvent*, because on my sunburnt skin
often, so often, I'd be trying to recall her touch.

Haiku! I'd jump up and yell to ships on the horizon,
recklessly reducing my limited supply to fifteen.

The marvellous *Murrumbidgee* flows 1,485 kilometres;
a Wiradjuri word English dries to 'plenty of water'.

I might see little *anatroccoli* obedient behind parents,
the Italian for ducklings lingering long on the tongue.

Rome also holds up *aquilone*, the kite I would make
to tug at the heartstrings of not-quite-freedom.

The solid English *steadfast* should check hunger,
loneliness, hold back the temptation to end it all.

Sine qua non, which I'd pronounce both sigh-nigh
and see-nigh. What's 'what-the-heck' in Latin?

A cheat? Sine qua non might look to be three words
but, as with people, without each other they're nothing.

---

* *Desert Island Discs* is a radio program started by the BBC in 1942.
Well-known people choose a limited number of songs or pieces of
music they'd take to a desert island. With words, the choices are
even greater.

First Hotel

Here in the deep red dark, the warm dark
there is no language, no sight,
no touch on skin, whatever that might be.
Within, merely sounds of plumbing
muted vibrations...notes?
obsessively these nine months.
Sometimes the craft does lose way,
as though we've been through a star-storm
and this sense of zero gravity,
the buoyancy, it falters;
we jerk from scheduled orbit.
Say she's eaten avocados again!
Or, leaving aside wine and smokes,
some mechanic palps, pokes,
often catching me shadow boxing
or training for the Tour de France,
and I take a stance, put my foot down.
Then one day, happily napping
after an in-flight refuel,
these kitten eyes lidded,
bells start ringing and, frankly,
it's like the end of the world.
Apparently it is the start
but picture a tennis ball being forced
down a garden hose!
The drag on ears, the flattening nose.

I'm told traumatic memories fade
as in an interrupted dream
but if so, how do I still have them?
The so-called primal scream?
I didn't say moo at the time,
the noise was all coming from Her,
caught between dilate and delight.
Here I'd ask, if I might, is it kosher
to clasp a fellow's ankles quite so hard?
to have one's peach-sized bottom slapped?
that mean clamp put on the fuel line?
and then to be wrapped
so tight in a rasping straitjacket?

This small packet
was wanting to shout blue murder
in the fluorescent-lit substitute 'room'.
I can report first uncoordinated hand
that when the light hit, smells hit,
my sound barrier smashed,
senses waving like an anemone,
someone laid my head on a skin pillow
and a warm bumpy device
– without any addiction advice –
was gently inserted between thin new lips.
Also that the first word to enter
ears once wonderfully deaf,
the in-the-beginning word, is 'Itsa!'

Some of the shocks were pleasant
 – if you've not gulped milk, gummed nipple –
but if anyone had taken the bother to ask,
I'd have stayed on
in the all-included, five-star
Hotel Mother.

Foothills

Those days in the foothills to France
our Catalan *nits d'estrelles*
and fruit blushing by the shed wall
fall to us heavily from here
our own skins awrinkle
in the portents of autumn.

I measured those days
through a square of glass
and still I see the tough grass
around the generous fig,
the boulder, smoothed by the Ter,
I levered below the pine we planted
for him
after digging out the wept willow.

That window welcomed night,
rain's tears down the talcum of dust,
the hens before the rogue dog,
the hallelujah of stacked firewood,
Gich's poplars, now-green now-silver.

Then's poem yellowing,
I revisit the pale boulder,
explain there's no need
to pretend permanence.

If Not More

'Beauty is one of the few things about which Cro-Magnon man knew as much as we do.' – Arthur Koestler in *Drinkers of Infinity*

Our cave here is comfortable enough
Sandy floor, dry walls
Danger of rockfalls
But the Dordogne weather isn't too rough.

All our children wear well-cut bison flay
The wife does good fire.
I'd like to retire
But she says I'd only get in the way.

So it's keep on clubbing, set trap and snare
Long days in the woods.
I know all its moods
Its smells, sounds, small changes in the air.

My favourite time is Muyt, when the leaf dries
And comes down the tree.
It is telling me
Light one day won't open my dawn eyes.

The wife points out some leaves stay green all year:
'Life might continue
At least for the few
Who obey Sun and Moon laws while we're here.'

I'm not much of one for such discussion:
Water where it flows
Fire to warm toes
A wall for art, tight skin for percussion.

The offspring want us to move up a rung
Modernise the cave
Like the neighbours have
Cook with wood, not dried buffalo dung.

I preach to them, as any father ought.
Beauty, I explain,
Dwells not in the brain:
By a deer, by snow, by sunrise be taught.

He lived about 20,000 years ago, his remains found in 1868 in Cro-Magnon Cave, France. His large cranial capacity is said to make him analogous to today's European.

Ingredients

Olive oil
rough-cut loaf
cold stream

Warm breeze
empty beach
rough-cut sea

Stone wall
evening
blackbird

Bees, ants
scoring
for the team

Four legs
dangling
off a pier

Old trees
believing
new leaves

Breasts
fulfilling
hungers

Flame's bright
welcome
+ farewell.

Personal Geometry

Right angle:
The tight corner where two walls meet
up there to the right of the blackboard;
the place reserved for dunces.
One day, neither the first nor last,
I was put there not for poor spelling
but for passing to another child
(do you remember this, Simon Holland?)
a scrap of paper where I'd scribbled
bugger.
I think I just liked the way adults spat that
word when things went wrong.
Teacher prodded me into the angle,
teary, ears burning to sniggers;
a fate worse than 'the cuts' from the head.
Time taught me to handle the third degree
but those 90 still scald, a lifetime later.

Parabola:
In Spanish, *para* means for, *bola* is ball,
as slang, a *bola* is a barefaced lie.
When executed by Professor L. Messi,
a parabola becomes a true miracle:
Force is applied to a round object on grass,
it loops over a wall of sweaty young men
holding their genitals, in the unlikely event…

Object begins negotiation with gravity,
curves down deceptively to where the Devil,
on a warm evening in Barcelona,*
does his utmost to keep it away,
punching, kicking, making theatrical dives.
The sphere curls past him to where Heaven
has assumed the form of small squares of rope.
Messi points up to God's weekday home.
Hallelujahs from the masses.

Parallels:
As with that pair of *ll*s,
parallels can never touch.
Euclid declared as much,
forever side-by-side,
equidistant to eternity.
Train tracks can seem to be,
deceiving via parallax or *trompe l'oeil*,
but true parallels play no trickery,
together-apart, if by millimetres or miles.

This love between us is unparalleled;
we travel together through life's flak
each with our private angles,
diverse trajectories, complementary ways.
When we embrace on these equilateral days
I like to think old Euclid would be smiling,
hands parallel then not, parallel then not.

---

* Lionel Messi has since moved from Barcelona to PSG.

The Hunter Home from the Hill

did not see death on its travel,
spiralling from his long thin tube,
its velocity almost alibi,
fortunate his eye can't accompany
what seems to arrive without passage,
a hairline crack in the cold morning air.

The gruntled pigs, the Bolshoi deer
know his priors, so he must hide
with his tricks: camouflage gear,
scope Galileo couldn't have imagined,
downwind for his killer smell.

For ducks, flak over the marsh
to hit wing or breast, steal flight,
cause ungainly splash
and the dumb dog's slobber.
The tiny balls that miss rain to the mud,
seeds of the ubiquitous Lead plant.

A shot is 'clean' when the dying
doesn't require thrashing through scrub
on splintered bone, glutting blood.
The term 'dirty' shot is not used.
Putting-out-of-misery, dispatch…
euphemism a hollow-nosed bullet.

Home from the hill,
hot showered,
the hunter cleans the long barrel.
Only his pillow might quarrel.

Title from Stevenson's 'Requiem'.

The Imperfect

Trying to live with the imperfect:
dovevo, dovevi, doveva, dovevamo…
is worse than the forgotten past:
ho dovuto, hai dovuto, ha dovuto…
After class I parrot slowly then fast,
forever unsure where perfect lies.

Not in the future, I like to surmise,
its nagging *dovrò, dovrai, dovrà…*
or in homework present:
devo, devi, deve, dobbiamo…
Before long one starts to resent
so many ways to decline 'must'.

'To choose' is a popular infinitive
though choice is more often mirage.
Its imperfect hurts mouth and mind:
sceglievo, sceglievi, even *sceglievano*,
third person plural, where I don't go.

'Love' lies in the imperfect,
and in conditional it belongs.
It's blurted in imperative *Ama!*
in those Eurovision songs.
But love's toughest tense, we know,
is *passato prossimo*.

Gained in Translation

Thai being tonal, the online translator
gets tongue-tied,
confounded by 44 consonants,
vanquished by 28 vowels.

The computer has the man say,
'I'm going to run away
from the doctor to cook
food for me to eat.'

The voice of the woman:
'If it's crazy,
we need to be crazy more than it.
You will know.'

He claims he is wearing
'two consecutive pants',
adding, 'the shirt is stuffed,
four layers of water.'

The woman concludes,
'It's time to lose the world.'

Pursuit

Man is not the art he makes
nor art a creator of men,
both a breath, a wingbeat
which unembodied come
to find their passing form
the way the wide Zambezi
deep in Zimbabwe falls
or the rose's passion play
with blood the thorn annuls
Nightingale, thunderstorm
halo adorning eclipse
piano note no pedal stops
phrase which leaves no lips
until the heavy curtain rises
a black hole cedes to math
moon in water, ship in cloud
takes up the painter's brush
tightly tunes the tenor's throat
patterns the poet's cloth
Green shoot of chance
ripe fruit of breeze
the climb of light on sky
hummingbird's suspended dance
sight far beyond the eye
captives of their capture
paint and write and sing
in hot pursuit of rapture,
deaf Beauty's bells to ring.

Sestina

On this granite rock a little lizard lives,
I'd say only six inches long, and low.
Unlike me, roughly half torso, half tail
and boasting four pumping hip bones
with which to nip across the terrace, so hot,
whenever he or she alerts to a quick bite.

Just now I placed on the rock a bite
of my lunch, bending slow and low
to avoid any shock in our disparate lives
but with a flick of that disposable tail
it rejects lettuce; maybe mayo's not so hot
for lizards' gizzards, hearts, few bones.

We do like to bake here, warm our bones
in sunshine, the unfailing love in our lives.
I have many needs, clothes even if it's hot,
you, just soft scales from tongue to trick tail
and when winter again begins to bite
you go for the flowerpot, slot there below.

I name you Limbo, being so lithe and low;
call me Arthur for these arthritic bones.
While I sit by your rock on my round tail
I ask which of our vertical or horizontal lives
is better? Lately mine has not been so hot
but we all must chew what we chose to bite.

An ant just nudged you, but you didn't bite;
my lot's not so good with live-and-let-live,
we reach for guns, knives, fights that entail
ego and power, often blood, broken bones.
Lizards do tangle, tempers seemingly hot,
but not from hatred, you don't stoop this low.

The afternoon's slipping, the sun getting low.
Soon we will resume our so-different lives.
I wouldn't want to be you, Limbo, no bones
about that, those eagles and crows on your tail
while inside I have wine to sip, bread to bite,
friendship, though it can run more cold than hot.

Equating our hot lives to animals' cooler bones is
dumb anthropomorphism, but as day tails off I bite
my lip: Limbo just looked at me and, lo, winked.

Losing, Lost

Greyhound-shaped, no stomach after the operation,
he corners me at the old people's 'home',
keen for conversation, desperate to try to hold
some bits of his disintegrating 90-year-old brain.

Reading the paper to this skinny old priest
one can almost see his synapses light, then dim.
'Turn the page,' he says. Then, 'Only the headlines.'
Suddenly he asks, 'The hire car?'

Father V. was a Latin scholar, more educated
than these fellow 'residents' he once oversaw.
Now he is on a par with them, shuffles on a stick,
stands slightly apart in the dining room line.

Like all priests, he learned how to bridge gaps.
He smiles, says, 'We will resume our talk later.'
Recently he asked a visitor to take him for a drive;
he needed to confirm certain streets, buildings.

I like him, but wish it was not too late now to say:
'In 1954, a girl of 11 came to the church to "confess"
– far too scared to tell a soul in her family –
what her uncle had done to her one day in his shop.'

And you told her
'Pray for him.'

Optional Third Lines of Five Syllables

Those who do haiku
enjoy cutting to the bone.
Don't have much to say?

      or:

That's done. Cool. High five!
Takes blood, sweat and tears.
Averse to long verse.
The way of all flesh.
Seventeen's magic.
Is less really more?
Goodbye to all that.
Prolixity sucks.
Can't get a word in.
What I mean to say…

Nudged

A nudge, a tug, now slack again.
Sunrise eyes squint across water
that confirms the Earth is flat.
Nylon slacks across forefinger.

Words out here are monosyllabic:
boat, bait, bite, spike, gill, salt,
sky, swell, wait…
Reeling, a shape slowly ascends

free but caught by a dumb idea
it follows up the baitless barb,
undulating beauty entranced
by metal that would lock into lip

or be swallowed whole and rip
organs as the fine line is hauled
to thrashed drowning in dry air
or knifepoint on the scaly board.

Just on surface, the big flathead's
tiny brain or tremendous instinct
homes it down the slippery slope,
and the bare hook takes my eye.

Partners

The handle can't divorce the blade
hinges hold prisoner the door
outer space requires an inner
the rich can't get shot of the poor.

Seeds ever lust for dark soil
water for level goes insane
sky is held up by blue magic
loss takes the boast out of gain.

Stick won't work without carrot
moods go up and down like stairs
the rose wants blood on its thorns
eyes come in synchronised pairs.

Calves are born to the slaughter
swallows owe their art to the air
the sea and the cliff call it quits
and hope lifts the lid on despair.

Refreshed

Exhausted salmon
climb their birth river to die,
no salt in the wound.

High Church

Two crows caw grey sky
arguing about whether
heaven's a black hole.

Seconds Before

the train pulls out,
runway jumbo strives for air,
unconfirmed drops of rain
pucker powdered fields,
hate's bullet departs barrel,
the bird on the branch
tilts back its head,
water hits coffee grounds,
eggs scramble,
butterfly poses
on winter's pruned rose,
a hand cups from a stream,
newborn nuzzles nipple,
soap lathers,
money is given away,
last nail obeys hammer…

Seconds later,
mere description.

Out of Mind

My country…
Its friendly face is deceptive.
I watch over it from distance
like a wedgetail above the Nullarbor.
Three decades away, I still smell gums,
hear magpies, dream surf.

My country…
its white version made by the pink-faced,
who in their turn feared a yellow peril,
can be seen as a melting pot,
though most I meet go straight to sharks.
Lately, some who follow international
ask, *Offshore detention?*

My country…
so many cuisines, so many origins
– Skovron, Nam Le, Tsiolkas, Chong –
but who can write what We did
to a young man from Iran:
'unlawful non-citizen' Omid Masoumali,
who set himself ablaze on Nauru.

My country…
trapped him on an island for three years
exhausting his dream.
From Iran, his mother told the inquest
how her only son got his name:
in Farsi, *omid* means *hope*.

Omid, 24, set himself on fire in April 2016 before a group of UNHCR officials visiting Nauru. The findings of the inquest were released in November 2021. Coroner Terry Ryan said, '…it is more likely than not that Omid was indifferent to whether he lived or died… I consider that his actions were those of someone who had given up hope and felt powerless as a result his prolonged placement on Nauru.'

'unlawful non-citizen' comes from Australia's Migration Act.

Wanted (I)

Call him R, a wanted man.
Not by any country, not by police;
by men who would cut out his tongue.

R can no longer live in Myanmar,
the Nobel land from which Rohingya
have fled, or been raped, murdered,
had their houses burnt.
He lies low in a cold country,
where he can't find work
and nobody speaks Rohingya.
There is a dent in his forehead,
souvenir of a soldier's rifle butt
back in *Burmese Days*.

R agreed to be wired,
to enter a camp where people smugglers
cash in on Rohingya misery.
He wore a camera hidden in a watch,
another fitted into spectacles,
Thai police clever if sometimes crooked.

A prosecutor needed hard evidence.
R could have baulked
but the man who wears a T-shirt
scrawled with a call to the UN
turned up for the trial, spilled.

In a land of Buddhists
that Buddha would disown
his generosity remains unsung:
just a man putting life on the line
to save others:
plot biblical, protagonist Muslim.

R's evidence produced convictions at two trafficking trials…then he flew back into exile.

Wanted (II)

Far, far from Myanmar,
back in the cold, cold country,
in a small rural village
R is taken under wing.

A local pastor and his good wife
and by 'Uncle', an old man
so frail he must get about
accompanied by an oxygen tank.
The two hit it off with gesture, smile,
the urge to understand.

Having to travel to see a journalist,
R stayed with 'Uncle'
who next day put him on the airport bus,
handing him a small parcel.

'Uncle' went straight home.
And died.
The news quickly reached R
and the journalist,
a woman who has spent years
exposing the Rohingya genocide,
herself in the process.

On an intercity train
R opened the parcel.
Refugee and reporter,
their cheeks wet,
shared the sandwiches
'Uncle' had made.

Petra Garcia Prieto's 100th

In this posh hotel a pride of us sits
to a nouvelle cuisine lunch
trying to cast back 36,524 days
to May 15, 1915, a Saturday.

Your unmissed, long-dead husband
always said you were frail, sickly
but it's you getting the mayor's plaque,
even a certificate from the Vatican
thanks to your Opus Dei nephew.
Perhaps not having kids contributed?
That and the cutting out and sewing
all those shirts to sell after the civil war.

1915 saw you in good company Petra:
Orson Welles, Sinatra, Ingrid Bergman,
Billie Holiday and Edith Piaf,
(who *between* them lived only 82 years).
Saul Bellow bowed out at 90
Pinochet wouldn't go til he was 91,
but at 100 you're still not done,
memory better than many of us here.

You are off the actuarial scale, Tia,
still addicted to *Hola* magazine
and to plugging earphones into the TV
for the afternoon's never-ending soap,
appropriately titled *Puente Viejo*.

We toast you, *Old Bridge*,
tomorrow will be your 36,525th day.
God is busy elsewhere.

Fontaine

Sister, I count your losses:
You can't read, can't write,
barely follow cartoons on your tv,
are unable to use a phone,
tell the time on the watch you wear,
ride a bicycle, even walk fast.
Your money is in siblings' hands,
you've but an intuitive idea of sex,
you miss Mother more than all of us,
she who you followed about
like a heat-seeking missile.
These days you wonder aloud
if she's still drinking in heaven,
laugh and say, 'Too much whisky!'
At her funeral you announced, loudly,
'She can't get out of that box.'

But can one miss the unknown?
What's more, you might list advantages
over your querulous brother.
For one, you never make lists,
haven't paid a bill in your life,
can say flat 'No!' to whatever
without a jot of reasoning,
are freed of most concepts,
including politics, famine and war.
You do have one of wedlock,
based on magazine photos
of your adored Lady Di.
When I remarried you asked,
'Going to keep this one?'

Brain damage has not left you
unaware of difference, 'Taine.
'Can't have children,' you repeat,
looking to your crib of obedient dolls.
Repetition is always new for you,
your favourite subject our dead.
You and I have a routine
to joyfully do the list:
'Granny Betty?'
We point aloft, chorus, 'Up there!'
Next…
You never point down.

When a staffer brings the phone
you often burn me with monosyllables.
If you give me a break, chat,
I picture you in the expensive chair
that raises or reclines your bulky body
while you doze away the long hours
between dining room refills.

Despite the motor damage
that precludes fine movement,
the God you believe in
appears to have taken note:
Your own awkward fingers
can make the recliner function.

Who can explain
remote control?

The Third Eye

'In Zen the spade is the key to the whole riddle' – Daisetz Teitaro Suzuki

To call a spade a spade
makes a man half-happy
wood and steel made
for working hands
lever's favourite lover
ender of Neanderthal kneel
finder of new potato
worm's doppelgänger
none of the fork's sly tines
the pick's pointed anger
or the fussiness of the rake.

Fudaishi, wise man of China,
had a deeper take
fifteen hundred years past:
'Empty-handed I go, and
behold the spade in my hands'
which to those at his feet
must have provoked shock:
he might as well have said
'A rose is a rose is a rock.'

Therein lies the leap,
one Jung thought too steep
for the Western mindset
inundated by intellect
addicted to appearance
seduced by syllogism
dual to the death.

Inhaling an Eastern breath...
The spade is a turner of earth
turned by the turning Earth
predisposed to nothing
designated only in dictionaries
hide-and-seeker
smiling in the closed shed.

Call Fudaishi off his head,
as many have before, absurd
nihilistic, an old man
bereft of common sense...
but perhaps he heard
the wooden horse neigh,
saw the stone statue dance,
by illogical happenstance
beheld with empty hands.

Haiku version

With its face buried
in the dark earth, is the spade
a Yes or a No?

The Origin of 'Marital Bliss'

The python swallows everything, head to toe
breathtaking in its rapture, unhinged
designed and built to gradually
digest the lumpy bits
over time.

The Bible doesn't specify the species
that lay in Eden's untrodden grass
but the evidence would indicate
it was the perfidious python
that led the first couple
up the garden path.

Turdus merula

What a shitty name for one so beloved.
Danes call him *solsort*, which at least
evokes those liquorice-dark wings.
Swahili's *ndege mweusi* brings hedges to mind,
which is where you often find them, full-throated.
Brasil's *passaro preto* conveys quick departures,
as does *feketerigó* in Hungary.
Is Sweden's *koltrast* comparison to the thrush?
Malay is *burung hitam*. I'm sure they don't.
Con chim den sounds like he's gone from 'Nam,
that yellow beak sprayed Orange?
Chinese enjoy him here and now, *hēi niao*.
The valleyed Welsh somehow sing *mwyalchen*.
He flies by *merel*, *mirlo*, *merlo* and *merle*
in Holland, Spain, Italy and France.
Germans given the chance use capitals: *Amsel*.
The *kos* may help placate history in Warsaw.

Why does English offer nothing better
– given redstart, osprey, peregrine or lark –
to the opener of our days,
announcer of cool dark,
than blackbird?

Dished

His creed was
Hungry? Then eat!
Tired? Sleep!
Sex? Willy-nilly!

God dished him
Cholesterol,
Insomnia,
The dodgy prostate.

Ode to Red

This Red it knows its way around
Travelling down the roads of vein
Selling a dollar for a pound.
                Fooled once again!

It starts at mouth, that entry point
Where tingling palate trembling waits
Each tiny tastebud to anoint.
                It opens gates.

Now driving south on cruise control
Throat wants it to go slower, please
14 degrees of alcohol
                Puts one at ease.

But north's where Red is heading to
The action's all there in the mind
Synapses…what a motley crew!
                Some are now blind!

Some wag the tongue, some close the ears
Others prod fools to make passes
Some produce guilt trips, even tears
                On two glasses?

Last Train

As the 4.15 p.m. off-peak rattles itself out from Central
most passengers are old men who couldn't describe
with their eyes shut the clothes they are wearing.

A gutted voice announces the stations.

Aginford: a few veteran cyclists dismount,
expensive bikes and lycra,
before the train humphs off along the relentless rails.

Middlestead: the platform is neither short nor long;
some women descend, unmolested by hormonal looks.

Workingstoke: grey, it's where the old men look out,
relief upstaging nostalgia. No point getting off here.

Youngstown: where the line ends, heavy rock belches
from the high-rise flats and fading graffito orders,
Climb a tower of freedom.

On the narrow platform the old men mull about
in the late sun, here a limp, there a curved back,
uncomfortable, awkward,
until they notice everyone else is also travelling light.
They adopt boyish grins, not having return tickets.

The Corpse Position

If worn back and knees twist the path
of meditation, try the corpse position.
The advice is from Tom Henry,
back from a retreat in Dharamsala,
two months of total silence.

Western corpses are positioned
by total strangers, undertakers
who undertake to have us made-up,
powdered and pretending.
I've never seen one laid out on its side
though the defunct might have slept
that way for seventy years.

I know at once corpse is the way to go,
offer a Dalai Lama-like chuckle
to kinked spine, gardener's knees.
Arms slack by side, I ease into
the 'box' in which I'll go up
or down in flames.
Unembalmed, attending only breath,
– Life's forget-me-not –
I tick towards empty.
With the added joy, it needs be said,
of slowly coming back from the dead.

The Dark Side

Fairy tales and Pink Floyd
had us believe one side of the cheese
Moon is forever in darkness.
Truth is, half's merely unseen
because the Man takes the same 28 days
to turn on his axis as he does to orbit Earth.
It's called tidal locking by those who read poetry
through telescopes, astronomers.

The Chinese have now taken seeds
and silkworms to the side we don't see,
a nifty step for man,
a dubious leap for moonkind
if the silk is for stockings
and the seeds are for kale.

On my own axis,
dark side unseen,
I trust that science
can't ever analyse
the tides,
the locking.

The Mind's Cession of its Kingdom

The brain will rule, the heart obey
until comes a day of abdication
or regicide.
Reason, unable to abide itself,
lays down its tools
and feelings fool around.

On this cold hill,
the clouds as still
as that brown cow,
the wind down a burrow,
the dog danced off on its nose,
mind can tell its cash is spent.

This grass is new,
these trees feel the last of a sun
just like the first.
Any thirst is in the eyes,
tongue's held mute in mouth.
Silence proclaims the king is dead
for an afternoon.

Title from the poem 'Moor', by R.S. Thomas

On the Road to Barcarrota

Chocolate fields exhale into morning,
freshly opened into autumn's arms.
Sun-after-rain polishes the clods,
no stubble left on the face of farms.

Worms keep turning the furrows for free,
puzzled sheep ruminate on the fact,
their world now looks like trays of brownies,
the cows know better, the barns are stacked.

Squeezed in hand tired soil will crumble,
hungry roots have sucked hard on its wealth.
Seeds in sacks wait their turn to explode;
what babe considers its mother's health?

Good arable land needs to fallow
just as brains become blunt robbed of sleep.
These dark fields should rest under heaven;
too much sowing…one day nought to reap.

Typing World War II Letters

(i.m. Captain R.A. Usher)

There's a naked man fishing
on a Guadalcanal beach
one day when Japanese planes
have paused their bombing runs
and the US offshore big guns
are not plastering what remains
of the Solomons' vegetation.

His mind keeps casting to a wife
who is carrying the child
he left in her on leave,
convinced he won't die here,
desperate to receive
letters in answer to all his,
read by a censor in San Francisco
then re-routed again so far
to Ballarat, Australia,
where he'd gone on R&R.

Up the beach a soldier waves.
Fisherman drops rod and runs
thrashes Jeep along muddy tracks
passing combat-weary men
playing cards, cleaning guns,
who hoot to see the mail-grin
of a captain dressed as on the day
he was born, in Brooklyn.

The corporal delivers a batch.
Nude hurries to duckboarded tent,
table and chair he's making
from scavenged pallet wood
when he and his don't have to go
wading swamps to pinpoint
men awaiting letters from Tokyo.

He reads his swelling bride.
Months back he wrote his dreams
of having her every imaginable way,
one such 'in a Jap pillbox, they
only lock from the inside!'
(the censor let that info go).

He doesn't see his daughter
until she's nearly one.
Postwar, Long Island, NY,
they produce another, and a son.
H&S Battery, 4th Btn, 11th Marines
and Pacific islands slaughter
now fade to typical scenes
of late-started domestic life:
he gets a job, rents a house,
buys himself a car, a Riley,
goes dancing with his sexy wife.

His letters were stored in a trunk,
hers disappeared after the war.
I know she once posted him a cake
to Guadalcanal (and it got there!)
that he sang beautifully.
Little more.
The typing has been a son's fishing.
When she lifted the phone that night
her captain was 37, I was four.

After Guadalcanal, where he got a Purple Heart, malaria, and complained that his hair was falling out, Captain Robert Austin Usher and family returned from New York to Australia, where he had a job. He was killed instantly when a car in which he was a passenger crashed into the back of a timber truck in Western Australia on 4 July 1950, Independence Day.

Onward Soldiers

A man is running, mouth wide in scream,
towards a certain spot on muddy ground,
in his hand a heavy rifle, bayonet fixed.

Someone's shouting at him from the spot
words fired in an urgent garble,
something like '*Nein! Vor Over! Halt!*'

The surrender has been signed off at 5 a.m.,
the officers know all about the 11a.m. cease
but the fellow goes, or is sent, 'over the top'.

He doesn't stop. At 10.59 on November 11
machine-gun bullets stitch Henry Gunther,
of Baltimore, in the 'war to end all wars'.

Millions of other Henrys have met death,
so many civilians and animals are dead,
words, sense, faith…all is four-years-dead.

A century later, the hymn schoolboys sing
is still misunderstood, 'believers' marching
off to war, not *as*. Ever more Henrys waste.

Marginal Notes

As she got older, ever more lonely,
Mother wanted certain things.
Not only cigarettes and whisky.
Paintings. She 'discovered' young artists.
She also had a good eye for sculpture.
Some of what we called her excesses
we parcelled out after her funeral:
I got the bronze head of the African woman,
Louise bagged the tall wooden cassowary,
Victoria has the best beach painting.
Brain-damaged Fontaine asked for the tv.

Mother also wanted an Arts degree.
Depression, age, and whisky were obstacles.
She dressed up for university, loved it,
once wrote off her blue Celica at the entrance.
Some students snickered at her hand-raising,
lecturers bemused by so much engagement
from an old woman with a posh voice.
Essays, however, were a hitch.
Margaret had ideas, theories, arguments,
but getting them down... She delegated.
Victoria and I ghosted them, got okay marks.
Graduation Day, robed and mortarboarded,
Margaret MacLeod was an exultant BA.

I also got some of her prescribed texts,
which languished on my shelves.
Just now I've read her *Moll Flanders*.
Though it's not the done thing,
and in anyone else's hand I'd be bleating,
it's got Mum's marginal notes in shaky pencil,
a belated inheritance for a son who often
tried in vain to drop anchor on her enthusiasms.
The notes bring her back as much as her photo,
looking like a fifties film star, above this desk.

Here, on page 84, where Moll says, 'being now
a Woman of Fortune, 'tho I was a Woman
without a Fortune', Mother has pencilled, *Me!*
On 91, Moll says, 'I lay still and let him come to Bed'..'
Mother, who boasted a big libido, notes,
almost in Defoe's English,
She has slight inclination.
Elsewhere is pencilled,
Fool
Decision of necessity, not ideology
Circumstance not inclination.

She underlines a lot. Where Moll says,
'I packed up my baggage and put myself
in Posture for a Journey',
Mother, a physiotherapist, underscores <u>Posture</u>.
I think Moll just meant get herself ready,
but that very nitpicking thought burns:
I was always trying to straighten
a mother who life had bent out of shape,
who wanted from me just hugs, praise,
laughter and shared whisky.

I kissed her cold forehead in her coffin,
spilled anecdotes at her crowded funeral.
A marginal son.

Roll Over Bing Crosby

In Harlem, Lagos,
Uluru, people might dream
of a black Christmas.

Chutzpah

Irving Berlin wrote
the song. Funny that, given
Jews don't do Christmas.

Epithalamion

(for scientists Jesús and Berenice)

So many distances:
poles, north and south
X and Y chromosomes
yin and yang
peace and war…
But certain opposites
eternally engage:
light greets darkness
heat heals cold
fresh river finds salt sea
rain anoints drought
a man and a woman meet.

The forces are mysterious
but explanation is overrated.
Tonight we can set aside
science, forget physics
because we are in the presence
of what neither can explain:
attracted hearts.

Observers, well wined and dined,
we place in Jesús and Berenice
our belief in happiness.
Like all faith, it is a leap
but our two dear friends, well,
they both have long legs.

Let us stand upon our own
and raise our glasses
to Berenice and Jesús,
Jesús and Berenice.
the J for joy, the B for bliss.
To this tonight
we stand witness.

Read at their wedding reception in 2017, this version and in Spanish.

Swifts

Sixty or so swifts, smaller than
swallows, sit on a TV antenna,
neither coming nor going
but each tiny pilot knowing
another summer is bowing out
and Africa is calling.

They fly short laps of sky
ping insects, pose again
jittery as we are in airports
awaiting boarding call.
No luggage, nothing at all
but a fixed idea:
winter's for birdbrains.

There will be hawks
hurricanes, aeroplanes
cold waves on ocean black
loud geese on busy skyroads
as your tiny brain decodes
maps written in white and yolk.

Grounded, I stack wood to burn.
Be swift. Be safe. Return.

Walking Out of Tomorrow

(for Angela Gutiérrez)

Will you walk with me for a while
though the day is now on the wing
the sun is lowering orange sails
and only the blackbirds still sing?

We could climb up to the high rocks
lean our backs against their held heat,
they give it off like bottled sun
where the sky and earth like to meet.

We have about two hours left
of daylight that no longer burns,
the path's slow dust and quick lizards,
the creek silent frogs and green ferns.

Accepted, forever is fanciful,
hearts like clocks will unwind,
but when we walk out hand-in-hand
poor tomorrow falls behind.

Babylon and Everywhere

(i.m. Voltaire)

I have not made the little hills dance
nor put the ocean to flight.
I have not seen the stars fall down
nor the sun melt like wax.

I did dance on a little hill
privately in my youth.
I have added tears to the ocean
to persuade it from flight.
I can see the stars fall down
by dropping my eyelids,
then welcome back their light.
Who would want the sun to melt?
I've watched the moon hide it,
sighed relief upon its return.

I've been dry and unimaginative,
wet and overimaginative.
My 'oriental style' goes little beyond
the spring rolls at the Fuoc Chon.

But I have seen a Frenchman
put fools to flight,
his words as pointed as stars,
humbug melting away
in the sunshine of his wit.

He had not made the mountains and the little hills dance enough. 'His manner is dry and unimaginative,' they said. 'With him you cannot see the ocean put to flight, the stars fall, or the sun melt like wax. He does not command a good oriental style.' – Voltaire in *Zadig*, describing the complaints after the eponymous protagonist made a clear, simple speech before two sectarian factions in Babylon.

Turn, Turn, Turn

True confession: I can't screw any more.
For an active man it's as though a door
has shut; life won't ever be as before.

My wife says I shouldn't worry so much,
there are doctors and medicines and such.
'Why is it so hard a subject to touch?'

I went to a surgeon, he shook his head,
asked the hard questions, I didn't turn red.
'Age brings limitations,' is all he said.

I work in the garden, still pretty fit,
lift a bag of cement, wood I can split,
but no more screwing, it's tough to admit.

Arthritis the cause, the pain is a shock:
two fingers on my right hand tend to lock.
Screwdriver's dead in the toolbox. Fuck!

Ducks

(for Michael Leunig)

They invented water repellent
millennia before Gore-Tex,
duvets before Nordics dreamt of them.
They amphib on orange triangles
more functional than mere feet,
don't need scarves or hot drinks,
their lings follow so obediently.

It never rains on a duck's parade.
They manage to say everything
in a word we stole for fake doctors.
They are neither Daffy nor Donald,
have nothing to do with cricket
or avoiding punches.

They must dismiss us as run-off.

Flight Fright

Weight overtakes speed
as cabin crew in thick make-up
are tonging us hot towels.
We are 33,000 feet above
the caste system?
Inter versus Juventus?
Somalia's hungry white teeth?
a school of sardines?…
in our given corridor
among the aluminium birds
when the engines stop.

Woody Allen's on screens
Dutchman's on his fourth whisky
full-nappy kid's catwalking the aisle
her parents in denial.
Outside the matchbox loos queues
are extended by Mile High Clubbers
poking fun at comfort.

A 777-300 briefly glides
before push comes to dive.
Autopilot washes its hands
and the one just woken by the co-
has no joy with whup-whup alarms.
All systems down, as is the nose.

At 45 degrees the screaming grows.
We've 90 seconds or so to rewind
then fast-forward through
loves, losses, wrongs, pendings.
But I just stare at the spilling juice.
The image which should be God
is that of the eager gymnasts
coupling in the 'Occupied'
wondering if they will get there
before we do.

Verde que te quiero verde

Why does grass bother to grow
again and again
after slash and weekend mow,
after cows with rubbery lips
randy rabbits, greasy sheep
all rip, ruminate, then crap on it?

We insist it's greener elsewhere,
insult the planet's second colour
using it to mean betrayal,
that not-so-harmless smoke,
say snakes lie await in it,
let fools dig deep divots with clubs.

If Sky mislays the watering can,
fire crisps across it
or agents commit herbicide,
our crewcut companion lies low
then resurrects, resurrects
to re-dress so-called pleasant lands.

Bamboo and sugar cane
are its taller family members
but let some of that short green
tickle those bare feet, so white;
grass is resilience, ambition, hope:
Lorca was right.

Room with a View

'Those looking for an even closer connection to Dickinson can rent her bedroom for an hour at a time and see precisely what she saw.' – from *The New Yorker*, December 2016

Hookers of the heart
you will not see the lines
my nature wrote from me –
which came delivered on wing
and green and blue
and each encoded thing
is neither false nor true
but for its receiver reserved –

a leaf fell for this window
a wind bowed down that branch
such and such a way
and the sway in my chest
like that when death rode by
then stopped.   I did try
on scraps of Father's paper
spoke them aloud to this room –
neither false nor true
but a way of seeing beyond view
the inexplicable wish to tell
what I may have briefly touched
above the Amherst green
a wing in the wide, wide blue.

Private still in rank and in death,
long gone from this room by the hour
where what I might have seen
held less my eye than caught my breath.

Let There Be Dark

Rui has those rectangular beehives
but also makes some from curved slabs
he cuts from the cork trees;
they look like a giant's top hat.

I go to watch him centrifuge
the full combs and to buy in
our annual supply of his gold,
alloyed with lavender this year.

Once from one of his cork hives
he cut out a small rectangle
and inserted a piece of glass,
wanting to watch the sweet work.

Lacking several front teeth
and looking beside a hive
like a soiled bride, Rui laughs,
'They covered it with mud!'

For the patient orchid bulb,
the climbing moon,
children asleep, and honey,
let there be dark.

Word

'I would suggest to the reader that, without the aid of a dictionary, he attempts to define the word word.' – Anthony Burgess

It was there in the Beginning.
Everyone wants to have the last.
Who doesn't appreciate a kind one?
A word in your ear might not be
the word on the street.
If I give you mine, will you keep yours?

Burgess, language his lasting love,
had far more than he needed for novels.
He knew words sometimes die
(Buchenwald, a beech forest?)
or are reborn (viral, enormity, gay…)
and are subject to our play:
to a Cockney, *A Clockwork Orange*
means something impossible,
like hens' teeth.

Taking up the Burgess challenge,
I'm about to define word as a sign
which won't always point the same way
when, to my dismay, I see Eliot called signs
'the word within a word, unable to speak a word,
swaddled with darkness.'

I wish wordsmith Burgess was still around
to shine his light.
He'd have imagined that we'd succumb,
reach for the fattest book on the shelf.

Etymology is detective delight
but words like to breathe, to burgeon.
Take a random stumble in the Collins:
entelechy.
Mellifluous, embedded between
Entebbe (Uganda…hostages…1976)
and *entellus* (type of Asian monkey).
But what work is it doing?
Collins says Aristotle and Leibnitz
gave *entelechy* entirely different ends.

I bet Burgess knew the word.
But don't take mine for it.

The Burgess challenge is from his selected journalism 1978–1985 under the title *Homage to Qwertyuiop* (Abacus).

The Eliot is from 'Gerontion'. In the same stanza he refers to 'the juvescence of the year', for which Burgess chided him: better is juvenescence.

Fifth Wheels

The soul, said Elijah of Nantucket
to Ishmael alongside the Pequod,
is 'sort of a fifth wheel to a wagon'.

The fishy prophet must have meant
it gets stowed, a bothersome burden
that will merely weigh down travel

Until one day life hits another rut,
the wagon dips shoulder to a halt
and those still riding bemoan Fate.

The cry goes up, but the fifth wheel
has been damaged or lost, fallen off
on the journey West into the sunset.

We're no wiser than florid Melville
about the organ no surgeon will see
(we *do* know more about whales)
but Eli's image rings true: a wheel
requiring constant reinvention.

Monody for Maria
(i.m. Maria Torres Contador)

Many men here hankered
but you were not up for grabs,
your plans in invisible ink
rewritten sunny day by day,
pretty head in the clouds
where passing birds might see
your sound-barrier smile.

We sang the songs of science.
Long black hair did not fall,
scalpels wrote calligraphy
between your small breasts
down to where you still mooted
motherhood.
All for the good said oncology
and we, we talked you up,
white-cell lied.
You turned 30, chemo for cake.

Why take Maria, asked your father,
when the world is so full of foul
and there isn't a soul in this town
who didn't light up on your approach?

In the church, standing room only.
The priest read the standing orders,
admitted he didn't know.
Claimed you were with the God
you didn't bother.

We watched you driven off,
waxen beauty in a box,
wooden cross heavy on its lid,
your famous smile slipping
through our cells.

Broken Secret

A match put to a fuse
gently as a kiss
and as irretrievable.

He'd take it to the tomb
he always said, and now
shrapnel, gaping wounds.

Disbelief, denial, fury.
Dogs that slept
now bloodhounds.

What cannot be unsaid
unstitching the family
that boasted no seams.

500 Million Reasons

Born with a silver spoon, life's pace is perfect.
Silent days and silent nights, who needs ears?
Horns, yes, to charge out of the dewey grass
at no miles per hour; the fighting bull envious:
horns tipped with eyes!

Hermaphrodite, but, like us, self-incompatible,
your reciprocal copulation can last 10 hours.

Few enemies: the French, thrush, blackbird,
believers in slimy cures, cabbage farmers.

In hot weather you simply seal the door
of the mobile home and wait,
resume life some nice drizzly day.
Who can gainsay a run of 500 million years?

In return for a bit of lettuce you pay your way
more than canary, cat or dog,
on moonless nights laying paths of pure silver
so fairies returning home won't get lost.

Haiku for the Dead

They can do no wrong
nor repair any they did.
Now, mere onlookers.

Photos: life support
systems that work for perhaps
two generations?

In fields packed with stone
thin cypress trees allow room
for more sets of dates.

Pantoum

Religion is food for the mind
As each mind has a different taste
We choose one particular kind
Select one god, no time to waste.

As each mind has a different taste
– It's what the Dalai Lama said –
Select one god, no time to waste
It's so easy to be misled.

It's what the Dalai Lama said
Sitting so still and breathing mind
It's so easy to be misled
While searching for the perfect kind.

Sitting so still and breathing mind
There is no need for crusaders
While searching for the perfect kind
The world's so full of persuaders.

There is no need for crusaders
Some minds are set in disbelief
The world's so full of persuaders
Most creeds offer no light relief.

Some minds are set in disbelief
Heaven's on high, but can't be seen
Most creeds offer no light relief
For new business the Devil's keen.

Heaven's on high, but can't be seen
Faith's a donkey, needs to be led
For new business the Devil's keen
Where do we go when we are dead?

Faith's a donkey, needs to be led
Along the road away from Hell
Where do we go when we are dead?
So far, no one's come back to tell.

Along the road away from Hell
We choose one particular kind
So far, no one's come back to tell
Religion is food for the mind.

His Holiness the Dalai Lama wrote, 'Religion is food for the mind, and as we all have different tastes we must take that which is most suitable for us.'

Overburden

At the outer edges of feeling
frayed threads of fact
presume knowing;
quite an act,
but who are we fooling?

Each of us *is* an island,
connection, a notion quaint
enough in one,
is clearly undone in two.

The heart, it's true,
is a deep mine
the head's light machinery
can't explore;
tonnes of overburden
conceal the grains of ore.

Villanelle

(for Andy, Alan, Michael, Helen, Sandy, Stella…)

So far from the trunk of life as it grew
Friends, we're out on the 70s limb
Barked high up the tree, still leaf, morning dew.

It's out with the old and in with the new
Those in their 80s look even less trim
So far from the trunk of life as it grew.

Out on this limb there are birds, one or two
We're closer to sky, not all news is grim
Barked high up the tree, still leaf, morning dew.

We've nowhere to go and not much to do
Still in the race, if no longer the swim
So far from the trunk of life as it grew.

Robotics, bitcoins, we haven't much clue
The young suggest our lights are going dim
Barked high up the tree, still leaf, morning dew.

We don't have to work, nostalgia rings true
Warm in the sun on our 70s limb
So far from the trunk of life as it grew
Barked high up the tree, still leaf, morning dew.

Father

'...and the metallic din went up through
the waste spaces of the air.'

Cousin Ian writes from Perth that his father,
my uncle John,
had to fly to identify the remains of mine.
I had always assumed it had been Mother.

I did know it was 1950, Western Australia,
front-seat passenger, the driver unhurt,
that Mother – the three of us under six –
later had to battle for insurance money.

But she would cry if we asked about him,
the details. We grew up learning only
that it was instant, perhaps to do with
headlights on high beam?

After her own death I found out more,
read the coroner's report and a letter
to Mother from a woman at the scene,
kind Mrs Bourke.

Just now cousin, with his scientist's clarity,
reports uncle's account,
worse than all he'd seen in the Pacific War
he and Father had fought in:

'Bob had been decapitated by a jarrah log
on the outstretched and unlit trailer'
of the timber truck, crashed into from behind
as it hauled its heavy load at night.

Above this desk is a head-and-shoulders
photo of the man I never knew.
He is handsome, mid-thirties, smiling,
curly black hair already starting to recede.
Taking down the frame, I kiss the glass,
his intelligent forehead, his strong neck,
the lips that Mother knew.
I smile back at him as a son would.

I can imagine that jarrah log,
milled, planed and polished,
now a refectory-style table
where some large family
bow heads to say grace.

Quotation from *The Iliad*, after Patroclus has fallen, the gods having decided his life didn't matter much.

Yesterdays

They think they can just slip away
given there's always another coming.
Film with the volume turned down
like tinnitus, a background humming.
The office of lost, never found.

They believe they are safely dead
that each sunrise prints a full stop.
A new crowd is knocking to enter
the mind's overwhelmed workshop;
tangents once again defeat centre.

They lie deep within Jung's dark
but there is a way to trick time past.
Don't release, say, 5.10 yesterday,
one certain moment, hold it fast,
that feeling no clock can gainsay.

With winter sun littering the floor,
we curled on the couch, as we do,
me stroking one of your small feet.
5.10 again, alone. No, not déjà vu,
time returns, this heart's still replete.

All our yesterdays have lighted fools…
and a lesson of love is to let it go,
accept dusty death, all that's gone.
But we fools against the tide row,
hearts holding, holding, holding on.

Preparatory

There comes a time
when you think you have
the socks to see you out,
that this last car will
go the distance if, like you,
it's greased and oiled,
a time when lust might
just lie in the teary eye
of the beholder,
when the leap of faith
might become a step,
and soon, those who thought
they knew you will forget
to dust the framed photo.

Meanwhile, there are trees,
skies, seas, your kisses,
grapes born again as wine.

Una Domenica Qualsiasi

Pomeriggio, e la luce non è amabile.
Nel cielo gli aquiloni invece di colori
offrono una sagoma nera, minacciosa.
Gli uccelli muti sono nascosto negli alberi.
È la domenica d'astinenza,
la malinconia gonfiandosi.

Sullo sfondo si avvicina il crepúscolo
attraverso il quale la luce sarà meno crudele.
Sarebbe meglio chiudere le finestre, le tende,
tenere lo sguardo attento alla parete.
Le domeniche sono per pensare
a non pensare,
teste nascote sotto le ali.

Any Old Sunday

Afternoon, and the light's not friendly.
In the sky the kites, instead of colours
offer dark silhouettes, menacing.
The birds are mute, hidden in the trees.
It's the Sunday of abstinence,
melancholy inflating itself.

In the distance, the coming dusk
will make the light less cruel.
Best close the windows, the curtains,
keep the gaze fixed on the wall.
Sundays are for thinking
about not thinking,
heads tucked under wings.

Separation

Memories rage across the page
like bull ants at a barbecue
neither agrees to disagree
or winnow false away from true.

He says love was never given
that it had strings, or rather ropes,
for her the field was never level,
his Needs outpacing all her Hopes.

Words that once were bedroom soft
are edited by lawyers now.
Possession is nine-tenths of passion,
up in flames the wedding vow.

We who clapped, raised our glasses
caught mid-stream, we duck the blows;
damaged hearts will damage spread;
parting shots have long echoes.

Addiction

'Addiction and its structure either confer meaning to one's life or exist to disguise the absence of such meaning.' – from *The Biology of Desire: Why Addiction is Not a Disease*, by Marc Lewis, Scribe

In each day's darkening the closed circuit of the blood
seeks a way out, aware all the while that to abide
the groaning in the veins is the stuff of the steadfast.

There's no similar river, one without an eventual sea,
no clear way to escape its current, to swim from the rush
to calm eddies, begin again the climb through original mud.

Nearly all is red, the lights, stop signs, the thumping head.
To give and to receive have become as confused as needles,
crime and punishment might as well be written in Russian.

Tow-truck territory, multiple pile-ups in the dense fog,
cables stretched to breaking point, jaws of life on wreckage,
adrenalin spent by the bucket. Nuclear the collateral damage.

Hope's river runs dry.
It has been known to flow again.
That first incipient trickle, about enough for an ant's bath!
Then gradual refilling, the dark sediment settling to dregs.

Bittersweet

The tree gave only one lemon, year after year.
People used to laugh and scold:
'Dig that poor thing up'.
I remained faithful, watering in summer
on the baking back terrace,
covered it when the winter frosts were biting,
rid it of thrip, once a white fungus.
It stayed little taller than me.

I'd leave that single lemon for ages,
the tree looking so naked when, finally,
with due ceremony, I'd slice it for gin.

Then one year, nothing changed,
same seasons as ever,
a bumper crop. Seven!
I boasted, made visitors stop.
They stared confused:
Along with the magnificent seven,
on a low branch also hung…
an orange.

Twenty years later,
oranges and lemons get along
in my extended family.

A grafting error. Oranges now outnumber lemons, but are suitable only for marmalade.

Homage to Flat

'L'eternità è orizzontale.' – Antonio Tabucchi in *I morti a tavola*

The mirror's brave attempt at same,
maps, the way they level all lands,
cards dealt fast in a poker game,
glittering salt flats, desert sands.
Records, the comeback 33,
horizon and the iron's hot face,
soles of shoes and those of the sea,
a cricket pitch rolled hard for pace.
Manta rays, floors, cotton sheets white,
TV and this computer screen,
lake, puddle and pond, drumskin tight,
the billiard table's perfect green.

Vertical plays some heady games,
spires and rockets, tall bamboo,
redwoods, waterfalls, LeBron James,
giraffes and cliffs, ambition too.
But flat's what Pisa's leaning for,
it's each erection's supine end,
Everest will be one day, for sure,
time and gravity all things bend.
That baby in a manger lay,
straw put down for his stable bed.
Heaven's on high, the bishops say,
but how do we lie once we're dead?

Spreadeagled

Stevenson's old man
was laid out 'like a cross in the sun'.
This one is in a walled terrace
beside a huge palm tree;
me, naked on an old rug,
the sun dressed in a sharp blue suit,
only sparrows to refute world's end.

Whitewashing walls blinding white,
like that Italian poet who could write
'broken by the years, tired of the road'
I dumped my load of brushes and pots
and lay down as though to die
in fine company:
a sortie of soldier beetles,
one speculating lizard,
bees on rosemary.

Three-score-and-more parts
imbibe the given,
smile for the unluckier who live in
the north's groin-deep snow.
Before the sun lets go the day
I'll re-dress,
embarrassed by the naked idea
of resurrection.

The reference is to an Anne Stevenson poem about spring titled 'Resurrection'.

Summersong

(i.m. Damien Gray, 17.3.1969–12.9.1989)

Blackbirds tweak the slipping light,
dunes are rolled-gold bars,
the surf has done a good day's work,
soon the first pale stars.

A ship holds down the horizon,
gulls condescend toward sleep,
beach is miming desert,
the new moon's task is steep.

One last look, just one last look,
as the Man said on the cross,
at these so-solid strokes of paint
on the wide white canvas of loss.

Not Counting

Let me *not* count the ways, nor add up the days
of all these decades since you and I were fated.
Some figures, and words, are best untranslated,
so leave sums to taxmen, our eyes would glaze.

A love so fully tested needs few calendar marks.
Some years we miss our wedding day, May 14,
have no need to list the highs and lows between.
But yes! These eyes still light to original sparks.

Often we anticipate what the other's about to say.
As if by map, we've learned our moods by tone,
knowing instinctively to leap in or to leave alone,
strengths and weaknesses in unplanned interplay.

What will happen to this love when we're dust?
Ask not, just stay spendthrift in kiss and care,
shields to poisoned arrows, to hatred, to despair.
Only count me in. For the steel, and for the rust.

Not

It's not what you think
thumps defence to the jury
It's not what you think
laughs the moon to the cow
It's not what you think
claims the lion to the deer
It's not what you think
meant the wedding vow.

It's not what you see
…is it still there if you turn?
It's not what you see
optic trick, the sky's not blue
It's not what you see
horizon pretending flat
It's not what you see
imagine mirrors could speak, too?

It's not what you hear
on the drunken grapevine
It's not what you hear
about the rich and the poor.
It's not what you hear,
in the gush of the gossip
It's not what you hear
…policeman at the door.

Diminuendo

Frost ends a poem about a warbler,
'What to make of a diminished thing?'

Life is a thing that diminishes
to a full stop,
punctuated by the commas and dashes
we enjoy inserting in death's way.
As Spaniards like to say
Que me quiten lo bailao!*

What to make of it?
A tuneful diminuendo,
'a gradual decrease in loudness',
toward that which can't diminish,
perfect silence.

---

* Meaning a consummated joy, as in having danced, can never be taken away.
The Robert Frost poem is 'The Oven Bird'.

Coming Back as a Bird

I'd always said spring's harbinger,
a pilot to embarrass the Red Baron,
the holy hero of *The Happy Prince*.

I got older, started leaning Cormorant,
majority here on our wide river,
outvoting even the ducks.
Above and under it they doubly fly
then hang out in the sun to dry.
But…silent, those black feathers
oiled as Elvis's hair?
And certain people would declare:
'I always knew he'd end in rant'.

Age making us ever more comical,
now I'm putting myself down
for the one some call the avian clown.
Fast as a penguin under water,
also a brilliant air-swimmer,
triangular red beak like no other,
plus black, white, yellow,
a burrower rather than nester.
God must have been tipsy
when He designed such a jester,
Chaplin in technicolour.

No, leave the eagle to mere dominion,
Crow to his continual complaining,
Owl to the acquired taste of field mice,
Seagull to scream and scavenge,
Sparrow to crumbs of junk food.
It's the circus next life:
Puffin!

Acknowledgements

'Desert Island Words' was in the Proverse Poetry Prize anthology, Hong Kong, 2021.

'If Not More', 'First Hotel', 'Flight Fright' and 'Turn, Turn, Turn' were published in *Quadrant* magazine under the late literary editor Les Murray.

'Ingredients' and 'The Dark Side' appear in the anthology *Outer Space, Inner Thoughts* (Interactive Press).

'Pursuit' appeared in *Meanjin* magazine.

'Yesterdays' was in *Cordite Poetry Review*, issue 80.

'Losing, Lost' was shortlisted for the MPU International Prize in 2017.

'Nudged' was in the Newcastle Poetry Prize anthology in 2020. 'Seconds Before' and 'Father' were in the Newcastle anthology in 2018.

'The Third Eye', 'Typing World War II Letters' and 'The Imperfect' appeared in *Australian Poetry Journal*.

'Fifth Wheels' was shortlisted for the A3 Poetry award in the UK.

'Summersong' appeared in *The Age* newspaper.

'Marginal Notes' was Highly Commended in the Australian Catholic University Prize, 2021.

'Coming Back as a Bird' was in the Grieve Prize anthology, 2021.

Changes have been made to some poems since first publication. Some poems appeared in the earlier collection *Convent Mermaid* (Interactive Press).

Lightning Source UK Ltd.
Milton Keynes UK
UKHW020650190722
406066UK00009B/1105